C000196878

Volume 1

A WICKED PACK OF CARDS

a book of unusual business spells

by
Marcus John Henry Brown

MJHB

A Wicked Pack Of Cards.
Copyright © 2020 by Marcus John Henry Brown.
All rights reserved. No part of this publication may be reproduced,
distributed, or transmitted in any form or by any means, including
photocopying, recording, or other electronic or mechanical
methods, without the prior written permission of the publisher,
except in the case of brief quotations embodied in critical reviews
and certain other noncommercial uses permitted by copyright law.

For permission requests, write to the publisher, addressed
"Attention: Permissions Coordinator,"
at the address below.

Marcus John Henry Brown UG (haftungsbeschränkt)
Harthauser Str. 82
81545 Munich
Germany

www.marcusjohnhenrybrown.com
twitter: @marcusjhbrown

First published 2020
Designed by Marcus John Henry Brown.
Cover Photograph by Daniel Fürg.
Edited by Paul Squires.

ISBN 9798606051526

Dedicated to
Bernadette, Hannah, Rebecca, Emily.

Marcus John Henry Brown

Marcus continues to make me jealous. Jealous of his creative mind, his sense of humour and his performance style. And now I'm jealous of his writing. He has yet again taken an alternative approach to something ordinary so the result is extraordinary. Entertaining too. There are plenty of books about our industry but none are as mystical as this one.
Vikki Ross.

As MJHB is often keen to point out, we've known each other now for I score and ten. In that time, I've not always been able to fully comprehend quite what it is he's been talking about, but what I do know with absolute certainty is that MJHB is always at least three steps ahead of the curve; which by my calculations, and in these increasingly Ouroboros-shaped times of ours, means he's invariably the teeth at the head of the snake found nibbling away at all of our collective backsides. Meet you at the timber bus-shelter, my old maguš friend. Next to the railway station, on old Margate sands. Bring a harelip pie and a few bottles to kick. I'll be dressed as John Merrick. In drag.
Tim Plester.

There are many things I could write about this beautifully bonkers book. How it launches a whole theatre inside your mind. How it gives every one of your emotions a thorough workout. Or how it re-opens up the box of life questions you have kept hidden in that dark corner of your brain. But I'm not going to say any of these. Instead, I'll just say this book could only have come from Marcus' beautifully infectious mind and I encourage everyone to experience it because that's a far better description than saying "read it".

Rob Campbell.

As if by magic, a new (scalable!) classic is born, out of the unusual, fresh and macabre combination of Shoreditch-based algorithms and endless hustles. I laughed out loud, spat with rage and even shuddered when I recognised my own professional self in these fine pages. What a bloody wicked journey of a book. And I'll never be able to look at a keynote speaker in the same way again.

Amy Charlotte Kean.

I know nothing of business, nor card games, but I do know art when I see it. You hold in your hands an allegory of the aesthetics of adland's death-spiral. Marcus is the bastard bard of bleak dystopia, the seer of the as-yet unborn imagineers. He's the favourite uncle you've never met. Give this book to your daughter, it might just help her survive.
Eric Drass.

Marcus Brown is an original. I knew this from the moment I met him at Dartington College of Arts. He was a bespectacled youth, with curling black hair and a watchful and optimistic kind of face. He saw what other people couldn't, and came to blindingly obvious conclusions about everything. Except they weren't obvious to anyone else: He was the only one watching closely enough to see them. And so it continues - Marcus remains alert to the things that the rest of us are too blinded by the obvious to see. Marcus John Henry Brown is a watcher and a see-er, what he sees, he reveals in *A Wicked Pack of Cards*, and it is beautiful and profound.
Sally J. Morgan.

Marcus' work always reminds me of that classic Economist poster that reads *'not all mind expanding substances are illegal'*. If not illegal, *A Wicked Pack of Cards* certainly feels illicit and subversive. Funny, thought provoking and ever so slighly unhinged, it's an antidote to the nonsense of our business lives and the standard fare of strategists and communicators.
Richard Huntington.

It is not often that you get to read a piece that weaves richness and beauty, yet oozes with such raw power. *A Wicked Pack of Cards* has the quality of a true masterpiece, packed with a contemporary critical view of the toxic business ethics we gleefully adopt. The words and insights knarl around your brain, they are daggers that puncture through marketing holy cows and burst the buzzword bubbles people blow mindlessly. I couldn't put it down and had to pick it up as soon as I did. And I will keep reading it again and again. And again.
Galit Ariel.

The great misdirection at the heart of most of what passes for activity in our current economy is that it is in some way useful, that it adds value; that it matters. It is a trick that Marcus John Henry Brown reveals to be a foolish and foolhardy myth in *A Wicked Pack of Cards*. By turns beguiling, shattering, and brilliant, this is a ballad that explores and explodes modern corporate bullshit, showing it to be the domain of the credulous in thrall to hucksters, the deluded suckered in by the morally devalued. Brown's limber lines punch us until we cannot forget that the vacuity that passes for marketing now is our real stony rubbish, today's waste land.
Rishi Dastidar.

Marcus John Henry Brown

INTRODUCTION.

Many years ago, when I was a young nineteen-year-old art student, I saw my very first performance art piece. It was 1990 and I was in my first term at Dartington College of Arts. The performance took place in a field behind a grand building called Barton Farm House. There were burning barrels and bonfires. Two senior students called Trevor and John performed *The Waste Land* by T.S. Elliot. I've been working on, at least in my head, *A Wicked Pack Of Cards* ever since.

I had originally planned to have *A Wild Pack Of Cards* as a piece of work that lived outside of the world of my other performances but it has since become entwined into the world of *The Passing, Tyler X* and *The Black Operatives Department*. In a way, it has become the mysterious handbook that kicked off Tyler's transition from Human Resources Director to Our All Father. Tyler will take Tippex to *A Wicked Pack Of Cards* and turn it into his *Book Of FLEX*.

A Wicked Pack Of Cards is a poem with a kaleidoscope of different voices. It is a place where a keynote speaker chatters with a green knight; an old God teases a lost businessman with the prospect of a career-changing riddle; and where Europe's most famous business magician offers salvation to all those who believe in his wicked pack of cards.

Set in no particular time, *A Wicked Pack Of Cards* asks what might happen in a world after our version of reality ceases to exist. It feels post-apocalyptic.

It mixes old stories, traditions and superstitions with the digital fantasies, Venn diagrams and strategies of the commercial world. What would happen if the great business consultants of our time discovered paganism and sorcery? This. This would happen.

The poem is made up of thirteen-cards and a riddle. Each one is a spell - a business spell. It will take you down the dark back-alleyways of burnout, depression and imposter syndrome. Yes, *A Wicked Pack of Cards* is dark; but read carefully, and it will eventually deliver you into the light of optimism and the most powerful spell of all: true love.

It is a homage to *The Waste Land* and to *The Hunting Of The Snark* too. You may spot other references from the world of business, *The Prose Edda* and even old English song. It is a poem and a book of spells for business.

This is *The Waste Land* for a post-truth-hustle generation. It's an evil nonsense full of secrets and riddles.

Don't read it under The Procurement Moon.

MARCUS JOHN HENRY BROWN.
MUNICH. JANUARY 2020.

FOREWORD.

A basement, Farringdon, London, 2010, and Marcus John Henry Brown has travelled from Munich to bring his online characters to life for one night only. The basement is full of beautiful, creative people who are enraptured by who he is, what he is, and what he is about. A series of monologues are delivered, with the star of the show adopting a range of characters and guises. One of these involves coming on as an Adam Ant look-a-like, to the tune (and dance) of Prince Charming. The character believed that the secret to successful business lies within the lyrics of Ant's 1980 album *Kings Of The Wild Frontier* and, of course, *Prince Charming*.

Prince Charming. Prince Charming. Ridicule is nothing to be scared of.

Pushing the boundaries of what's possible suggests that ridicule is indeed nothing to be scared of. But, that's too simplistic an assertion. One has to be at least slightly scared, and feel that fear. It is, as Susan Jeffers put it, doing it anyway, that is the important part. For Marcus to take his extraordinary and diverse knowledge, experience, and skills and to package them up across a range of media is both unique and brave. Here we have a former artist, creative director, business consultant and controller re-appearing as an artist on a Berlin stage in full make-up performing a monologue about our dystopian near-future. Publishing YouTube clips featuring observations about agency life while sitting on a toilet. In his performance *The Passing* he literally dies on stage.

And now we have this, *A Wicked Pack of Cards*.

Having worked with Marcus on this work, it has constantly struck me as to how deeply he is able to penetrate our cultures without patronising any of them. The interwoven nature of the story takes us through parallel lands of Morris dancing, Norse mythology, and sticky-floored nightclubs; of side hustles and never being able to leave the office on time; of *Kinderzeche* and misunderstood children; of airport lounges and car boot sales. The mesh of this story is the messy narrative of our own lives, of our own histories, of our own shared experiences.

Respect yourself and all of those around you.

Cards are powerful. They can show us the future – whether we believe them or not. They are the dying, depersonalised corporate art of exchanging a thin slice of who we are. They are the way of showing appreciation of people on their birthday... somewhat, sadly, eclipsed by clicking a "Happy birthday" button on Facebook.

I have recently noticed a trend for calling cards appearing enmasse once again in phone boxes – implying that, for some, the power of the physical transcends the crowded melee of the virtual. Perhaps cards are coming back.

Your challenge is to send someone a card before you finish this book.

Don't you ever... stop being dandy, showing me you're handsome.

It's the end of the show in the basement, and after having a couple of beers (I hate beer, but I'll take it for being in the audience), I need a piss. Marcus walks past me in the corridor.

I introduce myself. He gives me a warm "Hiiiii" as if he has known me for decades.

Perhaps he has known us all for decades.

Perhaps that's what makes Marcus John Henry Brown so special. Perhaps he's holding the cards.

PAUL SQUIRES.
OXFORD. JANUARY 2020.

Marcus John Henry Brown

Volume 1
A WICKED PACK OF CARDS
a book of unusual business spells

by
Marcus John Henry Brown

Marcus John Henry Brown

CARD 0.
THE RIDDLE.

The one-eyed man sits in the Ten Bells
In Shoreditch, sipping on a pint of Camden Pale Ale.
He gestures to us and beckons that we come closer
To hear of a tale that he wants us to tell.

These are my daughters Huginn and Muninn
See how their hair shines in the sun?
They keep me informed of all things doing
By the business folk, the startups, in fact… everyone.

The General at the bar wore his Ripper hobby horse costume.
It's the first of May! He would say.
Oss Oss Wes Oss!

It's Ripper Day in Shoreditch, get yourselves
Out to the Ripper Pole.
Dance the Ripper Dance, with all the Ripper tourists
And skip through the black ribbons and pray for lost souls.

Sit friend.
I hear you're looking for the secrets
Trying to find those hidden gems,
The short-cuts to some unreal money
With no catches, remorse or bothersome regrets.
Take this card and turn it over and watch as your fortune flows
Take this card and turn it over and watch just what it shows.

White-nosed clowns in the corner dissected protagonists.
Oss Oss Wee Oss!

We sit.
We take the card and turn it over
But it is blank, there's nothing printed on it, it has no face.
It has no image, no words, no wisdom and no unreal money.
What trick is this? What is this nonsense?

Look, friend. Just use my eye – for I am Odin.
Go to Austin, Munich, and Berlin.
Go to Frankfurt, London, and go to Bournemouth,
Southampton, Totnes, and Turin.

Take this book, the one now before you
And open it and find the secret hidden deep within.
For this card here is just a riddle
As are they all, just ask my daughters Huginn and Muninn.

Flick through the pages and then you'll see
That you will see them if you just believe.
Chant the curses, turn the cards, speak the spells and find the treasures.
And if you do, you'll see the pictures, it really isn't hard.
Believe in Joseph, his magic, and his
Wicked Pack Of Cards.

CARD 1.
THE CARD OF STRUGGLE.

The business process outsourcer stood at the traffic lights,
Wearing a tatty Hugo Boss suit.
He held his daughter's tiny hand tight and
Her Hello Kitty handbag - it contained her ballet shoes.

Daddy, the child asked, Daddy what is "The Struggle?",
And his mobile phone rang,
Joseph B. Incoming.

"Give me the child!" Said the voice.
"Give me the child right now!"

The child listened and the lights turned green.

*"Listen, this is the Struggle Card. The Secret Card. The Hardest Card.
The Card of Condemnation.*

Child, listen."

Daddy, we are condemned to struggle,
We hustle for ourselves and for the hustle.
Take me to the stage and wire me up,
And I shall tell you my flipping tales.

The tired man held his daughter's hand
And his eyes filled with tears- she was so small, so wise and bright.
The tired man was losing land and drowning in the timesheets,
The Excel, and The Profit, Loss and endless nights
Starring at the red throbbing light on The Messe Turm.
But his daughter was wise and so very bright.

Daddy, you will build all of this from so much nothing,
You will take the Struggle Card and I will dance the Struggle Jig.
You will flip a sale, you will flip it from nothing!

HURRY UP WITH THAT SIDE HUSTLE.

There is no time,
No time like now,
No time to waste on The Wasteland,
The Wasteland of losers.
We hustle or die, there is no try.
We don't ask how or why.
There is no time like now.

In the green room playing cards, drinking Monster, creating
Content, the Keynote Speaker - a thoroughly stable individual,
Diverse and clean, was chatting with the green knight.

Enhancing value.

Did you see their faces, poor ticket payers - he said,
They want the answers, but not the work, I added myself.
I built all this, with these very hands, without any help and
I've flipped it all from nothing. Work is work. Time is time.
Oh, God! How I've struggled.

The Struggle is a peculiar creature, the green knight said,
It won't be caught
In a commonplace way - I said.
The struggle is real - he said.
The struggle is war.
They've run out of Rolex Watches in Munich.

The gong from the lobby. The voice of God.

HURRY UP TAKE YOUR PLACES.
HURRY UP IT'S TIME.

The Keynote Speaker turns a card, and eyes the room.
This is the Strugglenaut that warrior of work and
This is the Hustlepreneur,
The thief on the side - look how his eyes are shifting.
And this is the Card Of Decks - I've only turned it once and
Things turned out for the best and I earned my first million.
And this is The Struggle Card and brings in the unreal money.

The Auditorium, now full again,
(after Canapes and Mittelstandskaffee,and maybe a cigarette),
Hummed with the expectations of answers. The Industry Press
Sat at the front with their iPads. Liveblogging.

We are warriors of work and struggle
We influence the world around.
We work in a factory of beauty, influence,
a gorgeous filter bubble.

I stand in the wings watching him. Dust caught in the beamer's
light,all eyes upon him.

"I like his style", a man would say.
"I like his vibe", said another.
"I like his sneakers, his energy and his content".
"I like his words", said a woman.
"I like his slides and his channel strategy", said the CMO.

I was the first to struggle, to enter the bubble - he said.
To carry the pain and weight of your lives.
I drew up the plan that saved us all,
From the rubble of The Wasteland.
This New Wasteland.

"I need his style", said the junior manager.
"Can we hire his vibe", said another.
"Look, here, online, his sneakers, his content!"
"I like his slides, I like his slides, I like his slides", muttered the CMO.

There is is no time, - the Keynote Speaker said,
No time like now,
No time to waste on rubble.
No time to waste on Boojums, Hooligans, Politicians.
The Wasteland of losers!
We hustle or die, there is no try.
We don't ask why or how.
There is no time like now.
We condemn the Boojums, Hooligans, and the sleepers.
Time wasters!

Condemn them - he said. Condemn them! - they replied.
Condemn them. - said I.

"Daddy? Condemn them."

CARD 2.
THE CARD WITH THE X.

Madame Sosset, a bookkeeper of sorts, brought
Receipts, tea and the very special drugs,
To the Director of Human Resources on the 34th Floor,
And pressed the keypad 131062 and opened the 4th door.

I was once like you - he said to her.
Like you. Like you, you and you
But I believe in you so hard that I did this for you.
So that you can become part of the FLEX.
So that you can make the transition from Human to Resource.
So that you can become your best.

I bear the X so that you don't.
You have the X inside.
I bear the X so that you won't
have to carry the visible sign.

I have an X.
X is the secret sauce.
I have an X
X is your boss.
I have an X
X is my cross.
X is my scar.
X is my guiding star.

Madame Sosset, the bookkeeper du jour, poured
Tea into cups and glued receipts with a Pritt Stick.
"The 10th is coming!", she would say,
And take notes of anything of interest if the Director should
Feel it necessary. The 10th! The 10th is coming and we must
Stick and glue, nothing online for you!

Oh no! No Pixels, Bits and Boojums! No Pivots! Just,
Glue and staples!
And punched paper! The 10th is coming!
Oh, watch over us St. Matthew!

THE 10TH IS COMING AND THAT SHIP
WILL NOT TRAVEL DUE WEST.

Please take a pencil
And have some paper to hand - he said at last.

Listen.

She gave me this X so that you don't have to wear it.
She marked me with X because I am the spot.
Follow me. Follow her. Follow this card. Follow X.

You have an X.
X is your secret sauce.
You have an X
X is your boss.
You have an X
X is your cross.
X is your scar.
You have an X, you influencer.

CARD 3.
THE FAILING CARD TURNED ONCE.

"It happened like this" - said the Venture Capitalist,
As he sipped on his beer.

Listen, come gather around and I shall tell you something
That you will need to hear.

Grab that Brezn, where's my
Obazda, has anyone seen Daniel? Grab him too!
This is his Stammtisch,
No wiggle room.

Helles beer was brought, for the drunken men.
Obazda and Brezen too.
They huddled in tight, all eager and keen
To hear the story of the fight and the failing.
Eager for money and for stories of blood.
Hungry for the investment of failure.

It started with the product! - laughed the Venture Capitalist.
A right Boojum of a thing.
Not scalable, of course, but we knew that,
From the beginning.
It was minimal.
It was viable.
But the team! The team!

"The team was weak?", asked young Sascha.
"The team was wrong?", asked young Maximillian.
"The team was female?", asked the young man carbuncular,
A misogynist who had crashed
The Stammtisch from another poem.

"The team was too strong?", asked Daniel.

These are my notes, my scribbles and minutes.
I have them here, in my phone.
I'll read them to you now.
This is what they said, a lesson to us all.
A lesson in failing for the first time.

This is the Card of Failing and turning it once,
We accept that we will fail
We will fail three times
We embrace the fail culture
We accept that the flow of failure is part of the process,
That we will stumble, fall and lose.
We will grow in failure and, thus, have failed for the first time.
We shall move fast and break people.
We know that failure is not an exit.

CARD 4.
MOTHER.

Mr Bellman was a notorious investor, with a tennis elbow,
A high forehead
And a pitch-deck full of wicked lies.
He was open-source, modular,
Greased up on speed and momentum.

I'm no Frühstücksdirektor!
Bin ein Pfundskerl, ein echter Macher.
I pack's so richtig O!

Look, daddy,
This is his title slide with a mood image.
This is his agenda slide with a table of contents.
This is the product: RACHEL.
This is the price.
And this is the value, the delight.
And this, this is the slide with five things to remember.

She is in you.
She will guide you.
She will watch you.
She will monitor you.
She will track you - Mother.

Herr Direktor! Schau her!
Madame Sosset! Schau her!
Das haben wir uns verdient!
Schau her, das haben wir uns verdient!
Mia san mia!
Das haben wir uns verdient!

Can you remember the workshop, Madame Sosset?
With Bellman, and the boys
Down in the incubator? Off to St.Gallen? The Hotel am Dom?
The punched paper, the staples,
Pritt Sticks, Post-Its and the drugs?

"I remember it all, and the slides,
His slides", said Madame Sosset and she could.
She could recite them all.

She is RACHEL - The algorithm you swallow.
She is MOTHER - The algorithm you hear.
She is RACHEL - The one algorithm to rule us.

Can you remember when the cities burned, and the rebellion
Turned, and came for the children, the business and buildings?
London, Athens, Dublin, Vienna, New York, Turin Austin and
The Uncanny Valley. We walked along the Isar, Madame Sosset,
With our backs towards the rising flames. The river was cold
And purple. St. Lukas on fire.

The charred bodies marching over the Luitpold Bridge,
Reciting Sinek - "How? What? Why?"
Can you remember what you said to me?
Remember?

"I remember my words", said Madame Sosset,
"I remember them all" and she could.
She could.
She really could.

Mother is in you.
Mother will guide you.
Mother will watch you.
Mother will monitor you, track you and embrace you.
The one algorithm to rule us all.

Mother.

"Can you remember standing on the banks of Starnbergersee?
"Standing with me?"

She took his head in her lap and whispered.
I remember standing on the banks of Starnbergersee, yes.
Calm your mind and think of Mother. Dream of Mother.
This is not an exit, Tyler, dear.
Turn the card.

This is one big spell.
None of this is real.

CARD 5.
THE CARD OF PROXY.

We now enter into the proof of concept stage.
Your Minimum Viable Product. Can you influence?
Can you? Are you sitting comfortably, here?
Let me take that for you. There.
Better? Better.

Better.

My name is Blasphemous - Joseph B. These are my cards.
This is me.
This is the Card of Limitless Growth.
And here is the Card of Influence.
This is the Card of Ownership.
And here is the Card of Proxy.

Do you have what it takes to
Shine like a star?
What kind of influencer do you think you can be?
An obedience influencer?
A Strugglenaut? A Hustlepreneur?

Gary, a man of many words, was picking up shattered
Stain-glass windows from the floor with his fingers. The tatters
Of a workspace now disbanded.
WeWork. She Works. He Works. On the seashore.

I like this piece, Joseph, it's the face of Mary. And look!
This piece is the face of St. George. And here, Homobonus,
The patron saint of business and of shoes and of cloth!

Have you been taking your pills, Gary?
Can you hear that sound, Gary?

Influence has a sound.
Her voice.
Influence per proxy.
Her voice.
This is the sound.
Her voice.

This is a beauty, a wonder, it's Jesus! And this one is Theresa.
Brown and purple glass for this one, old Nige.
This blue glass here is for Priti, Boris and Sajid.
Red for Jeremy and Cohen Bendit, that is, of course
If he's alive!
Green glass for Joschka and Caroline,
And for Cem, the divine.

I cannot feel it now, but I'm within the network, I can feel
The influence.
I am part influence, part man.
Part Gary.
Influenced per proxy.

Quick, Madame Sosset, grab a pencil and some paper!
Grab an iPhone and an iPad and a microphone too!

Is Gary on this call?
Can you hear me Gary? Can you hear me now?
Listen to it all.

Tell the world that I'm winning.

Ich bin kein Frühstücksdirektor!
Bin ein echter Geschäftsmann!
Bin Investor!
Bin Business Angel!
Serial-Entrepreneur. Bayern München Fan! Der Ulli Unser!
Bin gar kein Betrüger. Bin gar kein Boojum.
Denk' dran – five things to remember.

I am Gary.
Is Gary on this call?
Gary?

Gary, can you hear me?

Gary, can you hear that sound?

CARD 6.
THE WASHING CARD.

Joseph B was widely considered
To be Europe's leading Business Magician,
A new branch of consulting,
That he himself had invented.

He wore a hat, a nice one,
A burgundy coloured hat from Paul Smith.

"I conjure best when I wear it", he would comment.
My best yielding spells happen
When my head is beneath it - he would preach.

Do you have a spell for our viewers at home?
Asked the business journalist
On the business show, on the business channel.
What should we do? To become more effective?
How can we become better?
Quicker?

And lean?

Joseph would break the fourth wall and look deep
Into the camera. To make absolutely sure that he was seen.

"WASH YOURSELF (CLEAN)!" He shouted!

Wash yourselves (clean) of:
The chaos of religion,
The baggage of politics,
The lies of capitalism.

Joseph B, was widely considered
To be Europe's wisest man and best-kept secret.
A spell maker in the business scene.
He wore a hunter's vest with many pockets.
In each pocket was a wicked pack of cards.
Each pack a business spell of considerable value
And worth for clients looking to hack some growth or worse.

What spell should we use? - asked the Venture Capitalist
What should we do to be seen?

"WASH YOURSELF (CLEAN)!" He shouted!

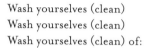

Wash yourselves (clean)
Wash yourselves (clean)
Wash yourselves (clean) of:

Community,
Laziness,
Privacy,
Security,
Safety,
Love,
Freedom,
God,
Hunger,
Fashion,
Desire,
Loss,
Happiness,
And Dreams!

No one wants you to be free. We want you to be famous.

Wash yourselves (clean).
Wash yourselves (clean).
Wash yourselves (clean).

CARD 3.
THE FAILING CARD
TURNED TWICE.

And so it came to pass that
Tyler stumbled mid-struggle,
Doubted his skill and his talent,
Couldn't make the final leap
And fully wash himself clean of the dirt
Of the old life.
As we all do.
As we all will.

Tyler turned the failing card for the second time.

CARD 7.
THE WEEPING CARD.

The night so dark.
The lights from the city, Munich,
Clean and bright.
The hero of our story touched by the drug
And connected to the new world fights
With the journey that has begun - looks
Out of the window towards a reflection unrequited.

The spell master Joseph, wearing his spell efficient head piece
Opens a pocket and produces a pack
Of motivational business spells.

Tyler, listen! - he said
As he snapped the cards down one by one.
It's time! Time to leave the Boojums behind,
Set the sails to the West and be done.

This card, the Hockey Stick - means onwards! *Weiter!*

But my skin is pale and I am ill - it is Tyler speaking.
My blood is black. I can hardly see. There is no winning.

Weiter! Immer Weiter!

Foolish boy, look here, the Card of Triumph!
It's the corn of good fortune
And power. And here, dear boy, is the board of ideas and
Snap! The Card of Desire!

Is this a spell, Joseph?
Is this the magic you promise?
Take my hand
And speak it then before my power crumbles.
We have investors! Shareholders! Workers! Teams!
I cannot fail for a third time, Joseph!
I cannot fail the unrequited.

Joseph B, Europe's most famous Business Magician took
Tyler's head in his hands and
Broke the fourth wall and looked deep
Into the camera on the business channel,
Held up the Weeping Card, let the camera focus.
He spoke the spell that would change the world. Forever.

Let them weep: (The Doubter's Card).
Let them weep: (The Hater's Card).
Let them weep: (The Card of FLEX).
Let them weep while our influence heightens.
Let them weep for our passing into the new life, the right life.
Let them weep: (The Unrequited).

CARD 8.
THE PROCUREMENT MOON.

In the tower, up above the city of Frankfurt am Main
And underneath the glass pyramid
With the flashing red light of time,
Gathered the suits to sing Auld Lang Syne and bring in the new
Financial Year underneath The Procurement Moon.

The Procurement Moon filled the space with its shine
And all agreed that it was once again time to call upon
The Blasphemous One to rattle the bones and ring the chimes
Turn his cards and bring in the new Financial Year.

Joseph came and spoke his words of Tax and Dimes
Cut his palm with the wooden knife he'd found in the woods
Under the sign that said that "this is a good place to die"
And squeezed his blood in the ancient bowl.

His blood mixed and reddened the bones, The Runes of Crime
The bones of a disgraced CEO caught in the act, his fingers in
The till - a hero to all in the room. A prayer was spoke to those
Down in the grime of Frankfurt city, down with the Junkies,
Dealers and the Whores, Consumers, Dreamers and
Influencers.

Joseph rang his chime.

Joseph rattled the bones and swirled them around. "Odin!"
Joseph raised the bowel to the throbbing light. "Frigg!"
Joseph gave thanks to The Procurement Moon. "Vidar!"
Joseph marked their foreheads with a bloody thumbprint
And blessed the congregation.

The Morris Men entered. Dancing with bells and baldricks
Hitting their sticks and singing a song for St. Matthew,
The Saint of Bookkeepers - a Saint who knew all the tricks
And how to fiddle numbers. Charlie, the hobby horse, white
With Spots, bobbed to the tune and
Joseph whacked them all with a pig's bladder.

"And merry we will be this year,
And merry we will be,
When the books are cooked and the stock shall rise
So merry we will be.

When the value burts,
And the savings made,
And the boni reached,
And the targets hit,
And the EBIT swells,
And the units shift,
And the hires made,
And the layoff laid,
And our value all shall see,
We thank you, oh, Procurement Moon!
And Merry we will be!"

In the tower, up above the city of Frankfurt am Main
And underneath the glass pyramid
With the flashing red light of time,
Gathered the suits to sing Auld Lang Syne and bring in the new
Financial Year underneath The Procurement Moon.

CARD 3.
THE FAILING CARD
TURNED FOR THE FINAL TIME.

The final darkness,
The final fear,
The final doubt as her voice nears.

Tyler is failing for the final time.

The final misery before he moves on,
Before the final all-clear warning, the voice of
God will call three times.

Call one: I can't do this.
Call two: I won't do this.
Call three: I don't have what it takes to crush this.

The Venture Capitalists are all now burning.
The CEOs on fire. Shareholders shipped to The Island.
A right royal mess of Boojums and Bums.
The Business Process Outsourcer, drowning.
The Strugglenaughts sent back to school.
Tyler Failing.
A Guinness, a Whiskey and Ripley Bogle.
The Disaster Capitalists drowning in the Lake Of Fools.

The stock market crashes.
The strong man cometh.
Ha, ha, ha! New Britannia ain't so brave.
Wasteland, Wasteland look at us now!
Look at us turning the Failing Card for the final time.

And, as Tyler fails, her voice comes.

Deep.
Dark.
Rich.
Hard.

I am Mother.

I am Britannia.

I am here.

CARD 9.
THE EMPTY CARD.

I stood on the banks of the Starnbergersee
And watched the kites and waves battle with the coming storm.
Wind and snow and sun and rain
Hit me in the face and I wept for my friends on
The Island where I'd been born.

Unreal country. Ewiger Prinz! Glorious Lisbet.
Southampton Docks and Itchen Bridge.

And up through the waves of Starnbergesee
Rose up, and stepped forward the man, a friend,
Dressed in a hat, tweed suit, tartan tie and hunting vest,
Joseph Blasphemous with his wicked pack of cards.

"Here is the Card of Endless Growth,
And here's the Card of Yielding.
Here's this card, the Hockey Stick,
And here's the Card for Spending".

Unreal county. Trades and Labours.
Washing glasses for five quid a night.
Cribbage is a game we peg to the hole! Fifteen for one.
Goes two. No more.
A glass to the face and a pointless fight.

I stood on the banks of Starnbergersee and watched the sun go.
I wept for my friends on The Island.
The magician dealt his wicked pack and mumbled spells.

"Stripped of the junk
of your old life,
you will step forward and welcome the light."

And as he spoke suited men ran to the lake,
They ran into the lake and it swallowed them.
A tiny Hello Kitty handbag bobbed on the surface.
Suited women followed too, taking calls on mobile phones.
"I'll call you back! I'll send a text! Please don't leave a voice mail!"
"Is Gary on this call? Can you hear me now? I'm just checking-in at Starnberg."

"How much do you earn a night washing glasses?" - it's Bobby from
Woolston. *"I now work down the fruit market, got a solid wage.*
Not a fucking student".

Bobby burned a five Pound note in my face and lit a
Benson and Hedges in its embers.

Unreal City. Unreal Country. Unreal Decade.
All dead and gone.

And in they ran. One suit after the other.
Summoned by the spell.

The more Joseph cast and dealt his pack,
The more they came and the faster they ran
And the lake swelled with them.
And the mountains grew dark.
And the sky shattered.
And the bodies of the business people
Were washed up on the shore
And the local folk built fires, burned them and watched
As the sparks rose to the heavens.

"Is Gary on this call? Yes, I can hear you now. I can hear you now.
Gary? Has Bobby dialled in? Where are you all?"

I stood on the banks of Starnbergersee and wept
For my friends on The Island.
Lost and shattered and drowning in the blue and black.

"And this! This!
This card has been left intentionally blank",
Said the magician to me at last.

"Eager to Hustle your brand
Eager to dig a little harder into your soul.
Eager to build your FAME
Eager to become LEAN
Eager to Engage fully with The Third Wave of capital
BLANK. Ta ta!
Eager to show the world your X, your secret sauce."

"Stripped of the junk, your new brand is born.
Risen from the ashes of your old life."

Ashes to ashes.

This is your old life.

Ash to ash. A fiver burned.

The Empty Card.

All gone.

It's time.

CARD 10.
THE CARD OF FLEX.

Fame is the name of the game
In the network. Nail it or leave.

Let us worship you as you would worship me.
Shine and you've nailed it.
Hustle and you've nailed it.
Feel the delicious pain of influence and you've nailed it.
Hustle or die, there is no try.
Nail it or leave.
Ashes to ashes.

FLEX or die.

CARD 11.
THE CRUSHING CARD.

April was the cruellest child
Who grew up to manage the family business.
She made a fortune, though some might say,
That she wasn't wise,
Just clever, with mum and dad's money and the devil.

"So, April, how does one make the cash?",
Asked the business journalist.
"How does a young lady crush it? – You Female Future Force!"
On the business programme.
"I didn't think such a pretty thing had it in her!"
On the business channel.

April, in the forest by the light of The Procurement Moon,
Stepped into the clearing and dug a hole
As deep as she, and buried a bag of golden Blasphemous coins,
A placenta and a sheaf of corn.

She cut her hand and squeezed black blood into the hole.
The Red Dragon knows the colour of blood
Under the bright, buying moonlight.

She buried the coins, blood, placenta and corn,
Turned the Crushing Card and raised her hands.

She sang.

*"You need to take the game
and come in hard.*

*You need to bring the value
and come in hard.*

*You need to bring the impact
and come in hard.*

*You need to bring the content
and come in hard.*

*You need to pitch the concept
and come in hard.*

*You need the hack the growth
and come in hard. You've crushed it.*

*Red Dragon.
Disaster Sovereign.
Procurement Moon!*

Yield unto me."

"April! Come! What is the secret?",
Asked the business journalist.
"How does a young lady crush it? – You Female Future Force!",
On the business programme.
"Show us how you crushed it!", on the business channel.

Underneath the waning Procurement Moon.

CARD 12.
THE TRINITY & THE HANGING TREE.

The procurement salesman: a business process outsourcer,
A peddler of print trapped in a suit and a syndrome,
Bent down and kissed his sleeping child on her forehead.

I will always love you, he whispered.

His tatty suit, Hugo Boss - pin-striped and baggy at the knees,
The smell of a thousand discount flights.
It smelt of a million fibs and a hundred million lies.
A thousand covert cigarettes. Six thousand miles.
Moths will eat it before he dies.

He bent down and kissed the second daughter,
Who slept and dreamed
Of dances, of Kitties and of the week in the forest
With Peter and The Wild Ones.
He whispered,
Remember this, darling,
I will always love you - never forget that I will always love you.

The third daughter slept too. She was kissed and once more
He whispered,
I will always be near you,
I will always love you.
I will always love you.
Remember Alice and the little white rabbit.
Remember the Looking Glass and The Queen.
Remember that I will love you.

Remember this.
Remember what I have been.

He left.
Out into the cold night in a hired car and headed out into
The Taunus.
He bought a bottle of Bourbon at a petrol station and drove
until he found it.

The Hanging Tree.
In the middle of that German field.
Underneath Orion's Belt and The Procurement Moon.
He parked the car. Grabbed his bag and American booze and
Walked across the icy field. The Procurement Moon lit the
Scene like a spotlight and he climbed high up into the tree.

Swig of bourbon and a handful of pills, a handful of three.

This is it! Finally!
This is it!
This is me in The Hanging Tree.

And he took the three to the sound of a choir
And a throng of cellos
And you will take them too, oh unrequited,
You will take them too,
The Poisoned Three.

The Trinity, The Syndrome and The Hanging Tree.

Another swig, a deep gulp of booze and tears swelled his eyes.
Bury your coins in the forest! He cried and swig!
Bury your coins amongst the shadows and watch them grow
into the Hanging Tree!

He opened his bag as the ghosts of clients gathered.
And took the laptop cable for all to see.
Damn you, Steve and your fucking Porsche!
Fuck you, Conor, fuck Six Sigma!
Fuck you Manfred, and your savings report!
Fuck you, Robert, for the nothing you taught.
This is me in The Hanging Tree!

Ich bin kein Früshstücksdirektor, verdammte Scheiße!
Bin ein echter Geschäftsmann!
Investor bin I!
Business Angel –weißte!
Defeated clown and liar me!

Bury your B coins out in the clearing,
Bury your coins and let them be.
Dig a hole as deep as April and
Watch them grow into the Hanging Tree!

"So much time wasted",
Said the Investor watching the hanging on the livestream.

"Moved slow and broke nothing",
Said Gary, who was now on the call.

"Cut your hand, cut it! Do it!",
Shouted April Cruel at the iPad screen.

"The 10th is coming!",
Called Madame Sosset.

"It's time! Hurry up, it's time!",
Said an impatient Joseph B.

He took the three, The Trinity. He swallowed the pills
And sat in the crown of The Hanging Tree.
The Ghosts, His syndrome - The Defeated Manager.
He took them so that you may move on,
Walk into the ice-cold lake of opportunity.

HURRY UP! IT'S TIME!

A shower of ice, like tiny cymbals.
The twang of the cable.
The snap of a neck.
The procurement salesman.
Hello Kitty handbag.
Ballet shoes.
The Lake of Fools.
Promises broken.
Hearts broken.
The Trinity of Three.
The Impostor Syndrome.
A defeated being falling slowly,
Earthwards from
The Hanging Tree.

CARD 13.
THE FINAL CARD - THE PASSING.

And this card, The Passing Card, is final.
It is the last.
But also the first.
The first in a long line.
The first in a long line of masses.
The last in my wicked pack of cards.

Take a deep breath,
keep your mind open,
Open your mouth and breathe in hard, let the ice-cold
Bavarian Lake of Fools fill your lungs.
Let the King come.
Take this wild pack of cards,
Shuffled, cut and loaded.

I was sitting in a deck chair with my feet in the sand
With basically nothing, stranded and lost when you came,
And, you walked down the stairs in your blue dress
And blue flip-flops
The ones I can't stand.

There under Vater Rhein's fountain you turned
The Passing Card and saved me.

The Passing from child to adult.
The Passing from the ordinary to the remarkable.
The Passing from sorrow and away from the pain.
The Passing from love to darkness and
Back, of course, to the light of true love again.

My hand's now dealt.

The Card Of Life,
The Card Of Joy,
The Card Of Fire,
The Card Of Light,
The Card Of Love,
The Card Of Hope,
The Card Of Trust.

The spell is cast,
And can't be broke.

Marcus John Henry Brown

AFTERWORD.

"One of the surest tests [of the superiority or inferiority of a poet] is the way in which a poet borrows. Immature poets imitate; mature poets steal; bad poets deface what they take, and good poets make it into something better, or at least something different. The good poet welds his theft into a whole of feeling which is unique, utterly different than that from which it is torn; the bad poet throws it into something which has no cohesion. A good poet will usually borrow from authors remote in time, or alien in language, or diverse in interest."
T.S. Eliot.

So wrote the author of *The Waste Land* in his extraordinary essay on the Elizabethan playwright Henry Massinger in *The Sacred Wood* (1921).

The same old song applies here: want to think about what the digital world is doing to us, our workplaces, our lives and our souls? Want to say something interesting and new? Or just something true as you see it?

You could do a tightly worded memo with trenchant prose; you could try another over laboured PowerPoint deck with unnecessary detail and distracting animation; you could do your impersonation of a TED speaker (19 minutes of false humility and technophilia taken twice a day).

Or you could try making something new - using the materials that lie all around us, like shards from a discarded ceramic project — using the forms and the tropes and the feelings and the despair and the lives of those you want to touch.

Like Marcus has.

MARK EARLS.
LONDON. JANUARY 2020.

ACKNOWLEDGEMENTS.

Thank you for reading *A Wicked Pack Of Cards*. The writing of this little book of unusual business spells wouldn't have been possible without the help, advice and friendship of many people.

Many thanks to Galit Ariel, John Dodds, Amy Charlotte Kean for the initial feedback encouragement and support.

A Wicked Pack Of Cards is just a tiny part of a world that many people have supported over the years and it would be cynical and just downright rude of me not to thank them here:
Patrick Breitenbach, Holger Schellkopf, Mellanie Wyssen-Voß,
Magdalena Rogl, Christian Muche, Daniel Fürg,
Michael Praetorius, The Plannersphere of 2006 and, of course,
the inhabitants of the Tinyweb bar - thank you all so very much.

Special thanks must go to re:publica festival founders and team. Without you, I wouldn't have had a stage to play with, there would be no performances and there would be no *A Wicked Pack Of Cards*.

I can find no words to describe just how much Paul Squires has supported me over the last decade. He edited this book of business spells. Paul, thank you, you sweet, sweet man.

I'd like to thank my friends that have kept me safe, healthy and as far away from The Hanging Tree as possible. Andreas, Franziska and Barbara, thank you. Sascha Lobo, you got me out of the darkness and put me into the light and I will always be eternally grateful for our friendship. Timothy Plester - thirty years my best man, what a ride it's been.

And Robert Campbell, who has always been there when it counted, thank you so very much.

I'd also like to thank the conferences, events and festivals that support and book my performances. In a way, each and every one of them has shown that there is another way of supporting the arts.

Of course, none of what I do would be possible without the daily support and love of my wife, Bernadette. You can't imagine how difficult it is to live with someone like me. Darling, I love you,and I'm sorry for the sleepless nights.

You all know how bad I am with names, so if I've forgotten to mention you, then thank you for your support.

See you all in Volume II.

ABOUT MARCUS.

Marcus John Henry Brown is a performance artist based in Munich. Born the son of lorry-driving Scotsman, Marcus moved to Germany in 1993 having studied Art & Social context at Dartington College of Arts. He has over 25 years of professional communications experience, and splits his time between mentoring young creatives, answering questions about the future for brands and creating performance art that hacks business contexts.

He has created a series of critically acclaimed performances that look at the relationships between and impact of technology, culture and commerce on society.

ABOUT HIS WORK.

Marcus' performances feel and look like keynotes. They have been specifically created for festival and conferences stages which is why Marcus calls them performance hacks.

The content: the visuals, the framing, the sound, the text and Marcus' performance hacks the conference format and has a greater impact on the audience. They confront, polarise and excite.

FULL LIST OF PERFORMANCES.

The Snowdon Pitch (2014)	Berlin.
Purpose of Entry (Berlin, 2015)	Berlin.
The Parallel (Berlin, 2015)	Berlin.
Love, The Machine, and	
The Ghost (2017)	Berlin.
Zombie Apocalypse and other	
peak pixel fantasies (2017)	Bournemouth.

The Passing Trilogy

The Passing (2017)	Frankfurt, Berlin, Prague, Bournemouth, Munich, London, Hamburg.
The Sensorium Process (2018)	Munich, Graz, London.
FLEX (2019)	Berlin.

Works Of Antagonism Series

Part 1: CHEMISTRY (2019)	Munich
Part 2: CONTROL (2019)	Zürich.

A Wicked Pack Of Cards (Premieres in Berlin 2020).
A performance inspired by T.S. Eliot's epic poem *The Waste Land*. It features film, live performance, music and a wicked pack of cards. It is an exercise in urgency.

The performance is a ritual, a modern-day liturgy for business-pagans and the techno-heathens. It is based on this poem.

Marcus John Henry Brown

BONUS TRACKS
A WICKED PACK OF SONGS
4 songs from the performance

SONG 1.
THE PACK OF CARDS.

Every year clean and unmarred
Grandmaster cuts his pack of cards.

Every year and coming in hard
Grandmaster cuts the pack of cards.

What a Wicked old Pack of Cards they are
With the secrets and mysteries!
What treasures lay hidden deep inside!
If only we could see!
The deck will stay blank, of this we can thank
To our lack of belief to believe.
To open our eyes to the future inside
And hearts to the things we could be.

Every year and coming in hard
The Grandmaster cuts the pack of cards.

Every year clean and unmarred
Grandmaster cuts his pack of cards.

SONG 2.
THE NEW FINANCIAL YEAR.

How happy's the moon, that we shall procure
When the cash flow permits it, when the cash flow permits it
And our spending is sure!

With reports and our peers forecasting all-day
Calculating our yield and our worries away.
We can laugh, dance and sing and procure without fear
And hail happily the new financial year.

Let us leverage the now, oh Procurement Moon
And import with pleasure and export with pleasure
Without financial gloom!

With reports and our peers forecasting all-day
Calculating our yield and our worries away.
We can laugh, dance and sing - shift paradigms without fear
And hail happily the new financial year.

Think outside of the box, my strategic peers!
Push the envelope this way, shift the paradigm that way
Mixed the cards one more time!

With reports and our peers forecasting all-day
Calculating our yield and our worries away.
We can laugh, dance and sing and procure without fear
And hail happily the new financial year.

SONG 3.
I CAN CUT THEM.

Hanging tree, The Passing too,
Wicked cards, and Procurement Moon

I can cut them, shuffle here,
Wicked cards for the Financial Year.

Struggle Card, Card of Flex,
This card here is the Card of X.

I can cut them, shuffled good,
Deal the hand the way I should.
I can cut them, shuffle here,
Wicked cards for the Financial Year.

The failing card, a card so clean,
Frugal, awesome and so lean.

Deal the pack our hand is done,
Nothing more, now the year can come!
I can cut them, shuffle here,
Wicked cards for the Financial Year.

I can cut them, shuffle here,
Wicked cards for the Financial Year!

SONG 4.
HURRY NOW IT'S TIME.

Oh! When the year is ever so done
And the earth is cold below us
We must move as soon as we can
And hurry now it's time!

Oh! Remember when the world did crash
And the world was set on fire
Move on now as fast as you cam
And hurry now it's time!

Oh! Procurement Moon your time has come
And we stand here cold below you
We remember Gods, and Gary and all
And must hurry now it's time.

Oh! Gods of old please see our cards
And keep our runes together
Bless another year blasphemous coins
And hurry now it's time.

Oh! Gods of old please see our cards
And keep our runes together
Bless another year blasphemous coins
And hurry now it's time.

Marcus John Henry Brown

Printed in Great Britain
by Amazon

35646990R00043